PHONICS LAND

BOOK 1

Single Letters

YBM

Book 1

Contents

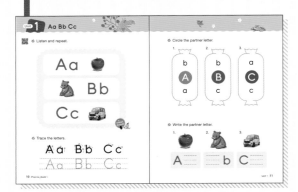

Letters and Sounds
Target letters and sounds are introduced with pictures.

Practice 1
Students recognize the pairs of the capital and lowercase letters and write them.

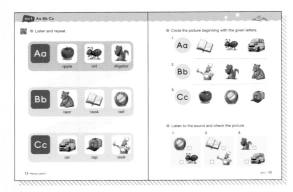

Words
Target words with the target letters are introduced with pictures.

Practice 2
Students practice identifying the beginning or ending letters and the sounds of the words.

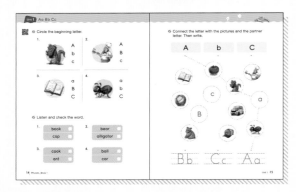

Practice 3
Students further practice identifying the sounds and the words by reading and listening.

Activity
Students are reminded of all the letters and words in the unit in the activity.

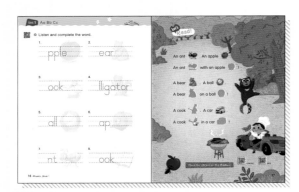

Listen & Write
Students practice listening the sounds of the words and complete the words.

Let's Read
Students practice the target sounds and words by reading simple phrases or sentences.

Review & Final Review

The review provides various exercises for all the contents of the previous four units. Students review the target letters and words from the four units. The final review provides a variety of exercises for writing and listening as well as activities covering all the target letters and words.

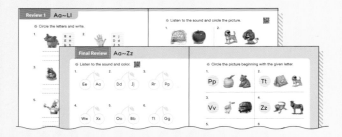

Special Features

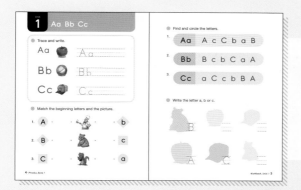

• How to use QR codes •

Scan QR codes on the content pages, then you can use all of the listening sounds and flash animations, such as chants, stories, and listening questions.

e-learning

Scan e-learning QR codes, then you can use e-learning for self-study.

game

Scan game QR codes, then you can enjoy the phonics games.

• Note for Teachers •

The ultimate goal of the book is to help students be able to read and write words even if they encounter a new word. Therefore, students should be encouraged to listen and to identify the sounds of the letters, not to memorize the spellings of the words.

✽ Let's sing an alphabet song.

Aa Bb Cc

Gg Hh Ii

Mm Nn Oo

Ss Tt Uu

Yy Zz

Dd Ee Ff

Jj Kk Ll

Pp Qq Rr

Vv Ww Xx

Now I know my ABCs.
Next time won't you sing with me?

❄ Connect the dots from **A** to **Z**.

❄ Connect the dots from **a** to **z**.

✱ Write the alphabet letters in order.

A B ___ ___ E ___

G ___ ___ J K ___ ___

N ___ ___ ___ R ___ ___

U ___ ___ X ___ ___

a ○ c ○ ○ f

○ h ○ ○ ○ l m

n ○ p q ○ s t

○ ○ w ○ y ○

✿ Listen and repeat.

A a

B b

C c

CHANT ALONG!

✿ Trace the letters.

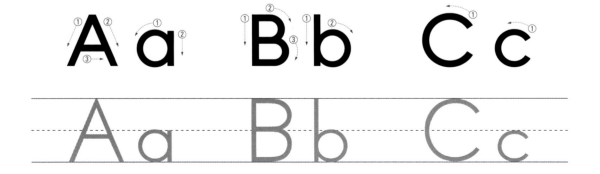

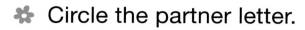 Circle the partner letter.

1.
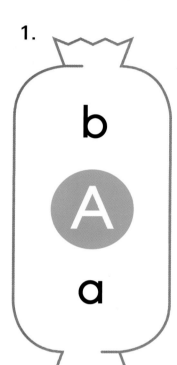
b
A
a

2.
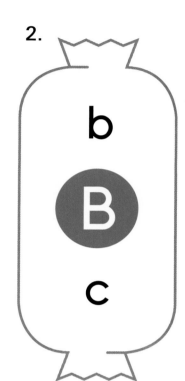
b
B
c

3.
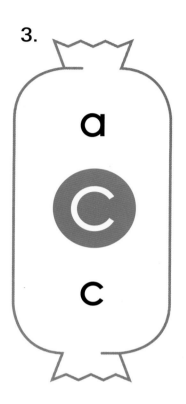
a
C
c

Write the partner letter.

1.

A _____

2.

_____ b

3.

C _____

✿ Listen and repeat.

apple   ant   alligator

bear   book   ball

car   cap   cook

✿ Circle the picture beginning with the given letters.

1. **Aa**

2. **Bb**

3. **Cc**

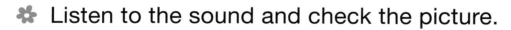

✿ Listen to the sound and check the picture.

1.

2.

3.

✤ Circle the beginning letter.

1.

A

b

c

2.

A

B

C

3.

a

B

C

4.

a

b

C

 ✤ Listen and check the word.

1.

book ☐

cap ☐

2.

bear ☐

alligator ☐

3.

cook ☐

ant ☐

4.

ball ☐

car ☐

❋ Connect the letter with the pictures and the partner letter. Then write.

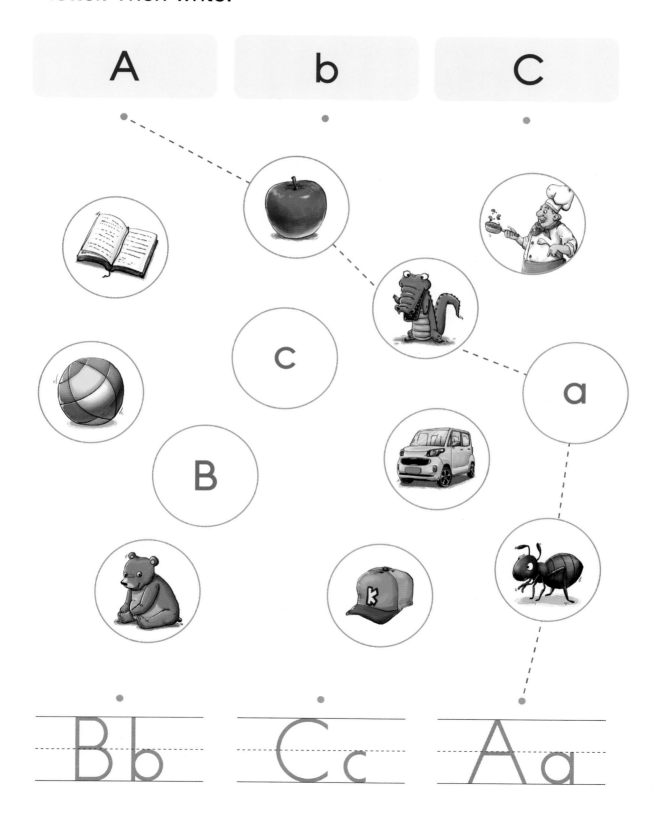

  ✿ Listen and complete the word.

1.

pple

2.
ear

3.
ook

4.

lligator

5.

all

6.
ap

7.

nt

8.

ook

An ant . An apple .

An ant with an apple  !

A bear . A ball .

A bear on a ball 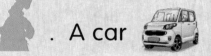 !

A cook  . A car .

A cook in a car  !

Place the sticker on the shadow.

e-learning   game

❀ Listen and repeat.

D d

E e

F f

CHANT ALONG!

❀ Trace the letters.

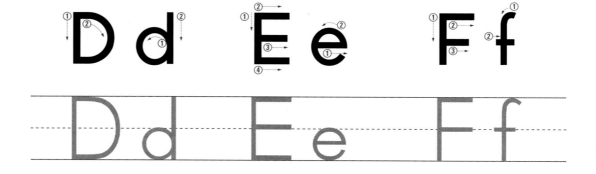

① D ② d ② → E ③ e ① F ② f

D d E e F f

❀ Circle the partner letter.

1.
D
e
d   f

2.
E
d
f   e

3.
F
f
e   d

❀ Match the picture and the partner letters.

1.   D   •      •   •   e

2.   E   •      •   •   d

3.   F   •   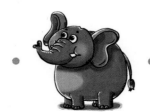   •   •   f

❋ Listen and repeat.

Dd dog duck desk

Ee elephant egg elbow

Ff fish frog finger

✿ Circle the picture beginning with the given letters.

1.
Dd

2.
Ee

3.
Ff

✿ Listen to the sound and check the picture.

1.
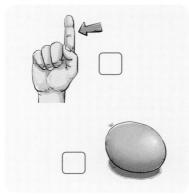

2.

3.

✿ Circle the beginning letter.

1.

D
E
F

2.

d
e
f

3.

d
E
f

4.

D
e
f

✿ Listen and check the word.

1.
dog ☐
elephant ☐

2.
egg ☐
fish ☐

3.
desk ☐
finger ☐

4.
duck ☐
frog ☐

❁ Help the bear find the apple tree. Circle the pictures on the way.

Start!

Write the beginning letters of each circled picture.

Dd → _____ → _____

🌸 Listen and complete the word.

1.

rog

2.

lbow

3.

uck

4.

lephant

5.

inger

6.

ish

7.

og

8.

esk

This is a dog .

The dog 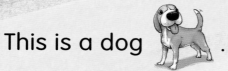 is on the desk  !

This is an egg .

The egg is on the elephant !

This is a frog .

The frog is on my finger .

Place the sticker on the shadow.

e-learning

game

✿ Listen and repeat.

G g

H h

I i

CHANT ALONG!

✿ Trace the letters.

G g H h I i

Gg Hh Ii

✿ Match the partner letter.

1.
G

I

2.
H

g

3.
i

h

✿ Write the letter g, h, or i.

1.

G

2.

___

3.

H

4.

___

5.

___

6.

I

🌸 Listen and repeat.

Gg

gorilla   green   grass

Hh

house   hippo   hand

Ii

igloo   ink   iguana

❀ Circle the picture begining with the given letters.

1.
Gg

2.
Hh

3.
Ii

❀ Listen to the sound and check O or X.

1.
O   X

2.
O   X

3.
O   X

4.
O   X

❀ Circle the beginning letters.

1.
G　　　　h
H　　　　g
I　　　　i

2.
I　　　　g
H　　　　h
G　　　　i

3.
H　　　　i
G　　　　g
I　　　　h

4.
H　　　　g
I　　　　i
G　　　　h

 ❀ Listen and circle the beginning letter.

1.　G　　h　　i

2.　g　　H　　I

3.　g　　H　　i

4.　g　　h　　i

5.　G　　H　　I

6.　G　　h　　I

✿ Match the beginning letters and the pictures. Then write.

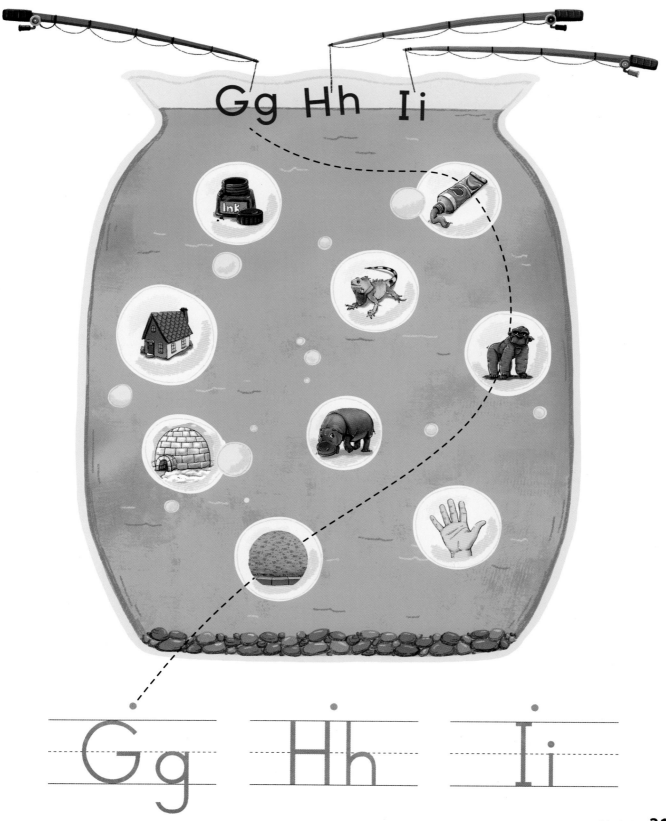

G g   H h   I i

 ✿ Listen and complete the word.

1.

_____ orilla

2.

_____ ippo

3.

_____ and

4.

_____ gloo

5.

_____ rass

6.

_____ nk

7.

_____ ouse

8.

_____ guana

Where is the gorilla  ?

The gorilla is on the grass !

Where is the hippo ?

The hippo is in the house !

Where is the iguana ?

The iguana is on the igloo !

e-learning game

Place the sticker on the shadow.

🌸 Listen and repeat.

Jj

Kk

Ll

CHANT ALONG!

🌸 Trace the letters.

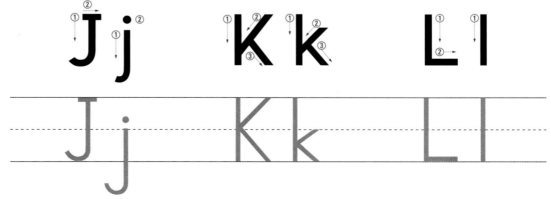

Jj Kk Ll

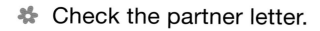

❀ Check the partner letter.

1 J ☐ l ☐ k ☐ j

2 K ☐ k ☐ l ☐ j

3 L ☐ j ☐ k ☐ l

❀ Write the partner letter.

1.

2.

3.

J _____   _____ k   L _____

❋ Listen and repeat.

Jj

jam   jet   jar

Kk

kangaroo   kitten   key

Ll

lion   lemon   lamp

✿ Circle the picture begining with the given letters.

1.
Jj

2.
Kk

3.
Ll

✿ Listen to the sound and check O or X.

1.
2.
3.
4.

1. O X
2. O X
3. O X
4. O X

❋ Circle the beginning letters.

1.
K   j

J   l

L   k

2.
J   j

L   k

K   l

3.
L   j

K   l

J   k

4.
L   j

K   k

J   l

 ❋ Listen and circle the beginning letter.

1. J   k   l

2. J   K   L

3. j   K   l

4. j   k   L

5. J   k   L

6. j   K   l

❁ Match the beginning letters and the picture. Then write.

K

k

 ❀ Listen and complete the word.

1.
_____et

2.
_____itten

3.
_____ion

4.
_____emon

5.
_____ey

6.
_____am

7.
_____ar

8.
_____angaroo

Do you like jam ?

Yes, I do. I like jets , too.

Do you like kittens ?

Yes, I do. I like kangaroos , too.

Do you like lions ?

Yes, I do. I like lemons , too.

Place the sticker on the shadow.

 e-learning

 game

✤ Circle the letters and write.

1.

B	e
E	H
b	h

_____

- - - - - - - - - - - -

_____

2.

H	j
D	d
J	h

_____

- - - - - - - - - - - -

_____

3.

C	i
c	f
F	I

_____

- - - - - - - - - - - -

_____

4.

J	D
L	l
d	j

_____

- - - - - - - - - - - -

_____

5.

E	L
e	c
C	l

_____

- - - - - - - - - - - -

_____

6.

A	k
K	b
B	a

_____

- - - - - - - - - - - -

_____

7.

L	j
k	l
J	K

_____

- - - - - - - - - - - -

_____

8.

G	a
C	g
c	A

_____

- - - - - - - - - - - -

_____

❋ Listen to the sound and circle the picture.

1.

2.

3.

4.

5.

6.

❋ Listen and circle the beginning letter.

1.
Gg   Aa

2.
Ff   Ee

3.
Kk   Gg

4.
Ii   Hh

5.
Bb   Dd

6.
Jj   Ll

✿ Listen and circle the picture. Then write the word.

1.

2.

3.

4.

5.

6.

❋ Find the beginning letters and write.

Gg Hh Aa Ee Ff Kk Ll Jj Ii Cc

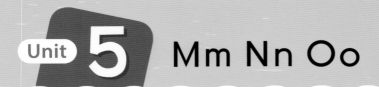

✿ Listen and repeat.

M m

N n

O o

CHANT ALONG!

✿ Trace the letters.

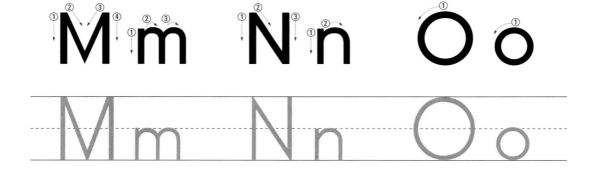

M m N n O o

M m N n O o

❀ Circle the partner letter.

1.

m

M

n

2.

o

N

n

3.

m

O

o

❀ Match the picture and the partner letter.

1.

 ·　·  ·　·

2.

 ·　· ·　· n

3.

 ·　·  ·　·

❀ Listen and repeat.

Mm

monkey   milk   melon

Nn

nest   nut   nurse

Oo

octopus   ostrich   olive

✿ Connect the beginning letters with the pictures.

1.

Mm • •  • •

2.

Nn • •  • •

3.

Oo • •   • •

✿ Listen to the sound and circle the picture.

1.

2.

3.

4.

✿ Circle the beginning letter.

1.

m
N
O

2.

M
n
o

3.

m
N
o

4.

M
n
O

 ✿ Listen and check the word.

1.
octopus ☐
monkey ☐

2.
olive ☐
nest ☐

3.
melon ☐
nut ☐

4.
milk ☐
nurse ☐

✽ Match and write the beginning letters.

 ✿ Listen and match. Then write the word.

1. **o**   • onkey

2. **n**   • strich

3. **m**   • est

4. **n**   • elon

5. **o**   • live olive

6. **m**   • urse

7. **n**   • ut

8. **m**   • ilk

What does the monkey eat?

The monkey eats a melon !

What does the nurse eat?

The nurse  eats a nut !

What does the ostrich eat?

The ostrich 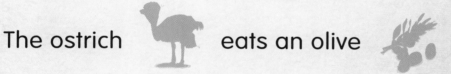 eats an olive !

e-learning   game

Place the sticker on the shadow.

❀ Listen and repeat.

Pp

Qq

Rr

CHANT ALONG!

❀ Trace the letters.

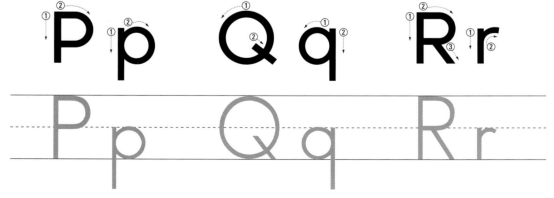

✿ Circle the partner letter.

1.
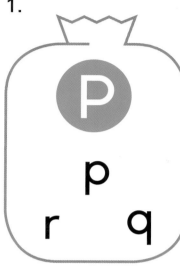
P
p
r   q

2.

Q
r
p   q

3.

R
q
p   r

✿ Write the letter p, q, or r.

1.

P

2.

3.

4.

Q

5.

6.

R

✿ Listen and repeat.

Pp

panda

pizza

pear

Qq

queen

question

quilt

Rr

ring

rabbit

robot

✿ Connect the beginning letters with the pictures.

1. **Pp** • •   • •

2. **Qq** • •  • •

3. **Rr** • •  • •

✿ Listen to the sound and circle the picture.

1.

2.

3.

4.

❋ Circle the beginning letter.

1.

P

Q

r

2.

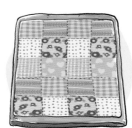

p

Q

R

3.

p

q

R

4.

P

q

r

 ❋ Listen and check the word.

1.

rabbit ☐

robot ☐

2.

queen ☐

pear ☐

3.

question ☐

panda ☐

4.

ring ☐

pizza ☐

❀ Help the mouse find the cheese. Circle the pictures on the way.

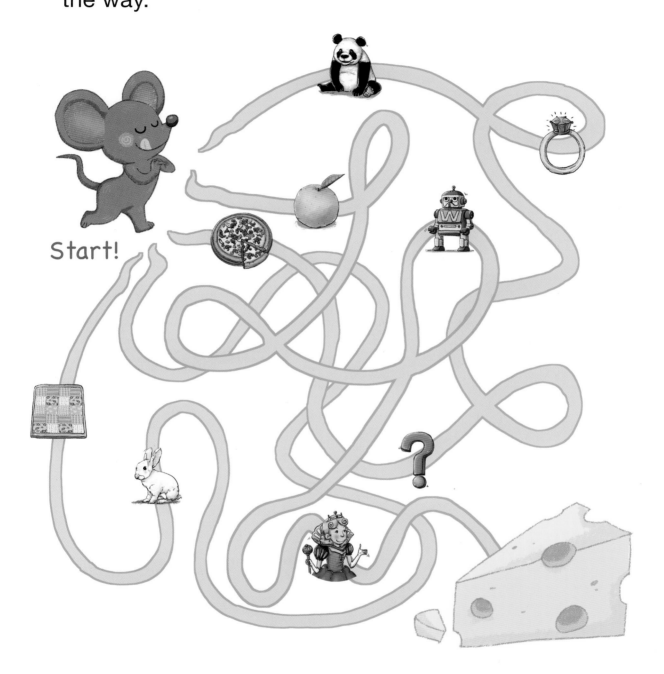

Start!

Write the beginning letters of each circled picture.

_____ → _____ → _____

 ✿ Listen and match. Then write the word.

1. **p** •   • ear _____

2. **q** •   • ueen _____

3. **p** •   • anda _____

4. **q** •   • abbit _____

5. **r** •   • uilt _____

6. **p** •   • obot _____

7. **r** •   • izza _____

8. **r** •   • ing _____

The panda makes a pizza .

It is very yummy.

The queen makes a quilt .

It is very warm.

The rabbit has a ring .

It is very pretty.

Place the sticker on the shadow.

e-learning   game

Unit 7 Ss Tt Uu Vv

❀ Listen and repeat.

❀ Trace the letters.

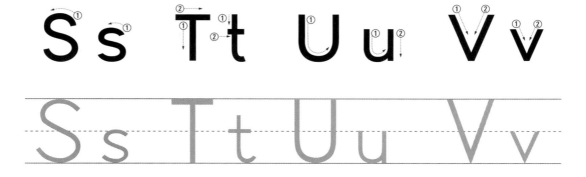

✿ Match the partner letters.

1. S

2. T

3. U

4. V

v   t   s   u

✿ Write the beginning letters.

1.  S

2.  _u

3.  t

4. 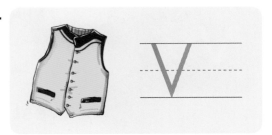 V

✿ Listen and repeat.

Ss

sock   snake   sand

Tt

tiger   tent   table

Uu

umbrella   up   under

Vv

vest   violin   van

Connect the beginning letters with the pictures.

1. Ss  

2. Tt  

3. Uu  

4. Vv  

Listen to the sound and check O or X.

1. 
O X

2. 
O X

3. 
O X

4. 
O X

✿ Circle the beginning letters.

1.
u   S
T   t
s   U

2.
t   V
U   T
v   u

3.
u   v
V   S
s   U

4.
V   s
t   T
S   v

 ✿ Listen and circle the beginning letter.

1. S T u v

2. s t U V

3. s T U v

4. S t u V

5. S t u V

6. s T U v

✿ Match the pictures with the same beginning letter.
Then write.

 ❀ Listen and match. Then write the word.

1. u   •   • iolin   _____

2. v   •   • iger   _____

3. s   •   • ock   _____

4. t   •   • nder   _____

5. u   •   • nake   _____

6. t   •   • ent   _____

7. s   •   • p   _____

8. v   •   • est   _____

The snake on the sock .

The tiger 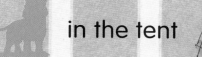 in the tent .

They are all mine.

The umbrella  under

the table .

The violin on the van .

They are all mine.

Place the sticker on the shadow.

 e-learning

 game

❀ Listen and repeat.

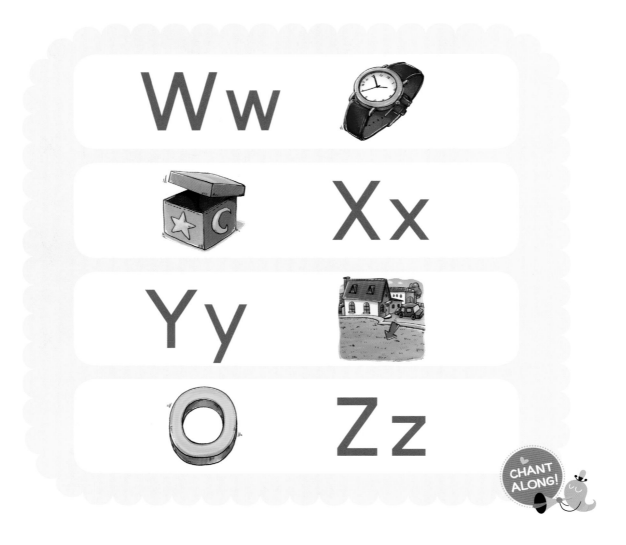

CHANT ALONG!

❀ Trace the letters.

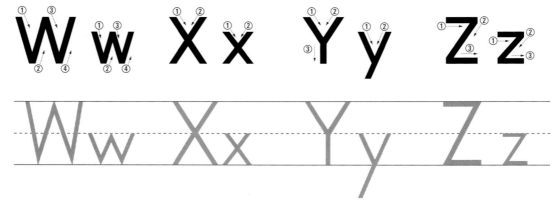

❀ Check the partner letter.

1. **W** ☐ y   ☐ **w**   ☐ x

2. **X** ☐ **w**   ☐ **z**   ☐ x

3. **Y** ☐ x   ☐ **w**   ☐ y

4. **Z** ☐ **z**   ☐ y   ☐ x

❀ Write the beginning or ending letters.

1.  W

2. X

3. y

4. z

✿ Listen and repeat.

Ww

watch   worm   web

Xx

box   ox   mix

Yy

yard   yacht   yogurt

Zz

zero   zoo   zebra

✿ Connect the beginning or ending letters with the pictures.

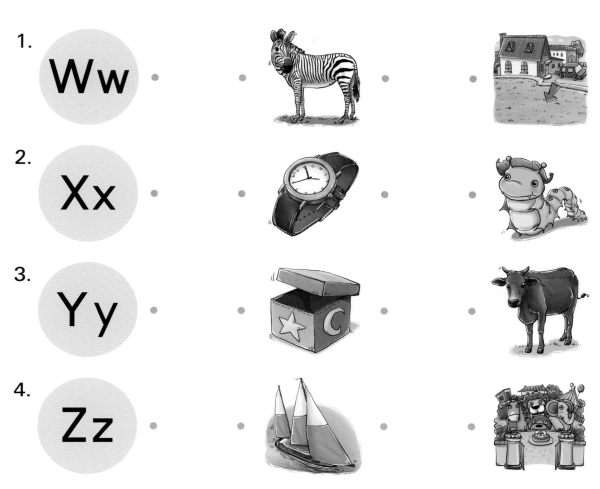

1. Ww

2. Xx

3. Yy

4. Zz

✿ Listen to the sound and check O or X.

1.   2.   3.   4.

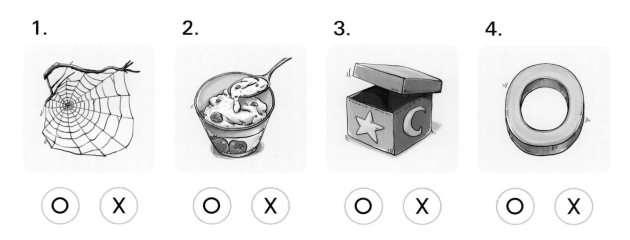

O X   O X   O X   O X

❀ Circle the beginning or ending letters.

1.
w   Z

z   W

X   x

2.
X   W

Y   y

w   x

3.
Y   W

w   z

Z   y

4.
x   z

y   X

Z   Y

 ❀ Listen and circle the beginning or ending letter.

1. W   X   y   z

2. W   X   y   Z

3. w   X   y   Z

4. w   x   Y   Z

5. w   x   Y   Z

6. W   x   Y   z

✿ Match the beginning or ending letters and the picture. Then write.

 ✿ Listen and match. Then write the word.

1. **w** •   • eb   _____

2. **x** •   • mi   _____

3. **x** •   • acht   _____

4. **y** •   • atch   _____

5. **z** •   • oo   _____

6. **w** •   • ard   _____

7. **z** •   • ebra   _____

8. **y** •   • bo   _____

A worm is in the web .

Two oxen is in the box .

Three yachts are

in the yard .

Four zebras are in the zoo . e-learning

game

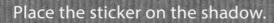 Place the sticker on the shadow.

❖ Circle the letters and write.

1.

S   P
W   w
p   s

_____

- - - - - - - - - - - - -

_____

2.

M   T
q   t
Q   m

_____

- - - - - - - - - - - - -

_____

3.

W   o
Z   w
z   O

_____

- - - - - - - - - - - - -

_____

4.

y   P
s   Y
p   S

_____

- - - - - - - - - - - - -

_____

5.

X   y
r   x
Y   R

_____

- - - - - - - - - - - - -

_____

6.

q   O
V   Q
v   o

_____

- - - - - - - - - - - - -

_____

7.

s   p
o   S
P   O

_____

- - - - - - - - - - - - -

_____

8.

v   Z
z   R
r   V

_____

- - - - - - - - - - - - -

_____

✿ Listen and circle the picture.

1.

2.

3.

4.

5.

6.

✿ Listen and match the beginning letter.

1. 　2. 　3. 　4. 　5. 　6.

| Uu | Qq | Zz | Oo | Rr | Pp |

Listen and complete the word. Then match.

1.

| | | l | | n | •

2.

| | | t | | i | c | h | •

3.

| | n | | | r | •

4.

| w | | | m | •

5.

| | o | g | | | t | •

6.

| | e | | t | •

7.

| b | | | •

8.

| | i | | g | •

❋ Write the beginning letters for the picture.

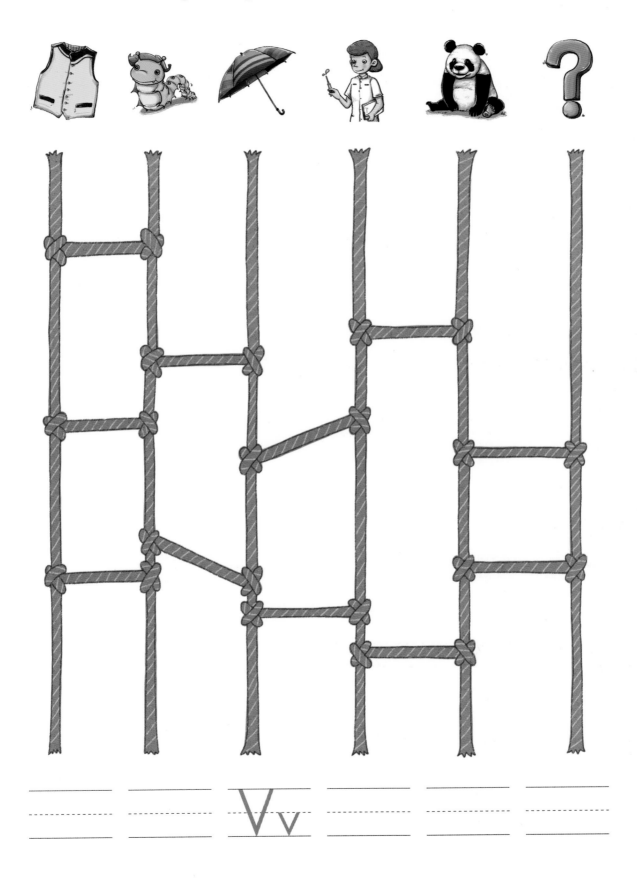

✿ Listen to the sound and color.

1.
Ee   Aa

2.
Dd   Jj

3.
Rr   Pp

4.
Ww   Xx

5.
Oo   Bb

6.
Tt   Gg

7.
Mm   Ff

8.
Ss   Uu

9.
Ll   Zz

10.
Cc   Nn

11.
Qq   Vv

12.
Kk   Hh

❋ Circle the picture beginning with the given letter.

1.

2.

3.

4.

5.

6

7.

8.

9.

10.

Listen and help the rabbit find the umbrella.

✤ Write the beginning letters.

_____

_____

_____

_____

_____

_____

_____

_____

_____

_____

_____

_____

_____

_____

_____

_____

_____

_____

_____

_____

_____

_____

_____

_____

_____

Period	Unit	Target Letters	Target Words
1	**Alphabet**	Aa, Bb, Cc, Dd, Ee, Ff, Gg, Hh, Ii, Jj, Kk, Ll, Mm, Nn, Oo, Pp, Qq, Rr. Ss, Tt, Uu, Vv, Ww, Xx, Yy, Zz	
2	**Unit 1**	Aa/a/, Bb/b/, Cc/k/	apple, ant, alligator bear, book, ball car, cap, cook
3			
4	**Unit 2**	Dd/d/, Ee/e/, Ff/f/	dog, duck, desk elephant, egg, elbow fish, frog, finger
5			
6	**Unit 3**	Gg/g/, Hh/h/, Ii/i/	gorilla, green, grass house, hippo, hand igloo, ink, iguana
7			
8	**Unit 4**	Jj/j/, Kk/k/, Ll/l/	jam, jet, jar kangaroo, kitten, key lion, lemon, lamp
9			
10	**Review 1**	Aa/a/~Ll/l/	
11	**Unit 5**	Mm/m/, Nn/n/, Oo/o/	monkey, milk, melon nest, nut, nurse octopus, ostrich, olive
12			
13	**Unit 6**	Pp/p/, Qq/kw/, Rr/r/	panda, pizza, pear queen, question, quilt ring, rabbit, robot
14			
15	**Unit 7**	Ss/s/, Tt/t/, Uu/u/, Vv/v/	sock, snake, sand tiger, tent, table umbrella, up, under vest, violin, van
16			
17	**Unit 8**	Ww/w/, Xx/ks/, Yy/y/, Zz/z/	watch, worm, web box, ox, mix yard, yacht, yogurt zero, zoo, zebra
18			
19	**Review 2**	Mm/m/~Zz/z/	
20	**Final Review**	Aa/a/~Zz/z/	

ANSWERS

Student Book Answers

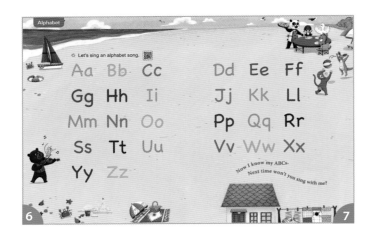

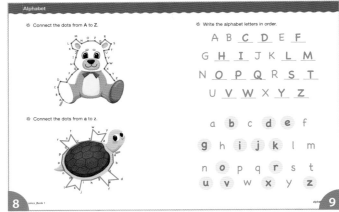

• Unit 1

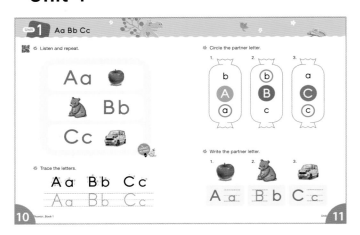

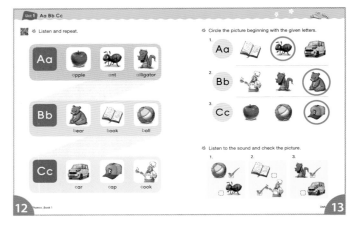

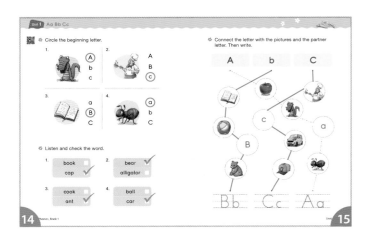

• Unit 2

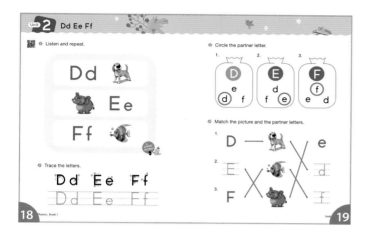

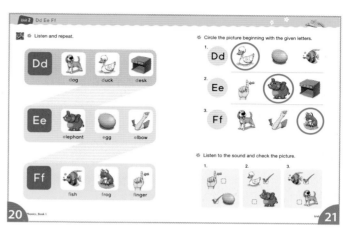

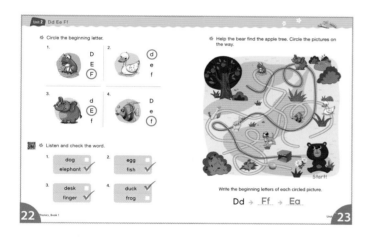

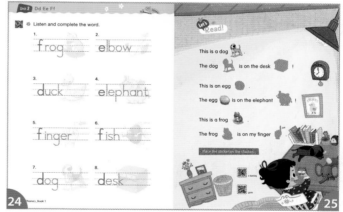

• Unit 3

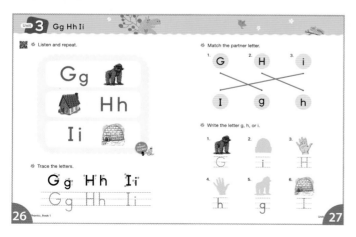

Student Book **Answers**

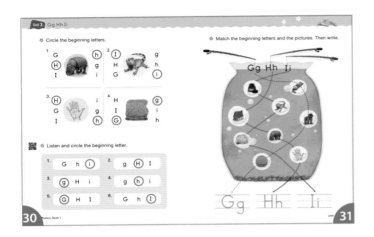

• Unit 4

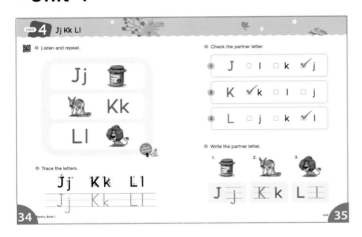

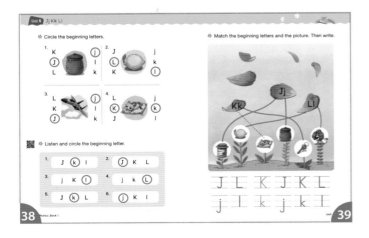

• Review 1

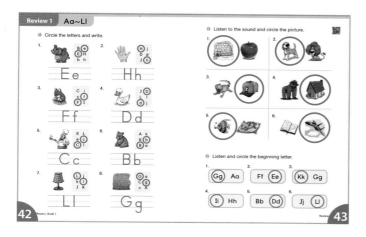

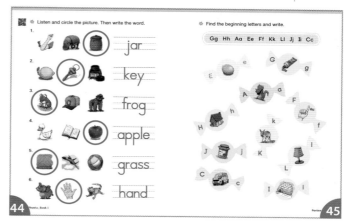

• Unit 5

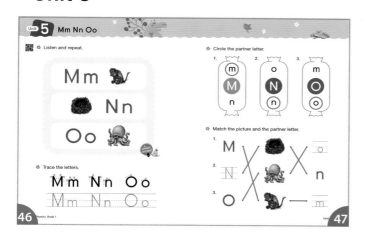

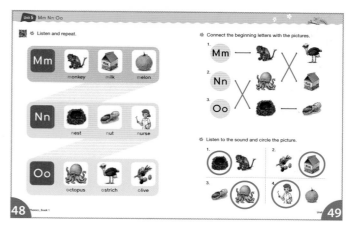

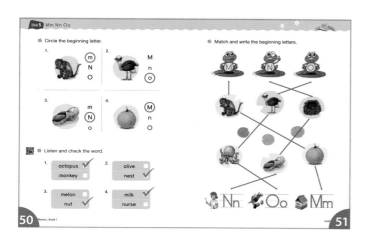

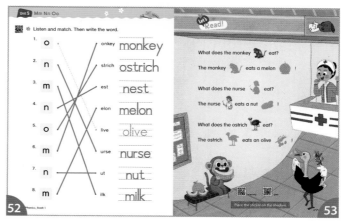

Student Book **Answers**

• Unit 6

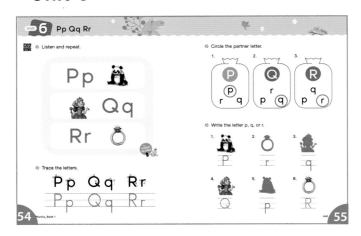

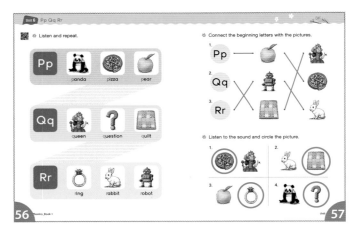

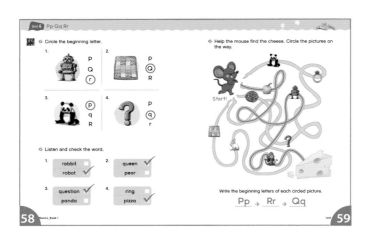

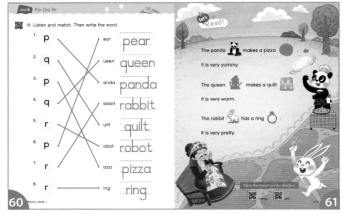

• Unit 7

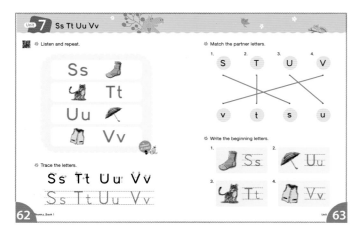

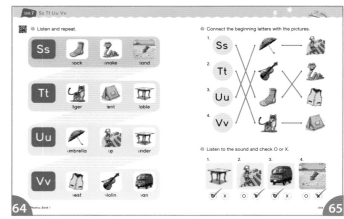

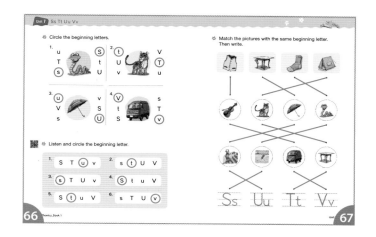

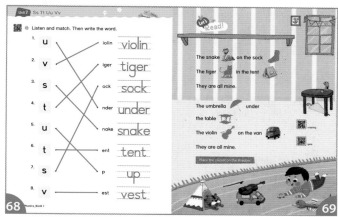

• Unit 8

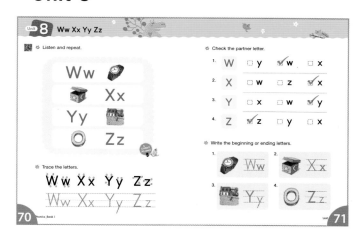

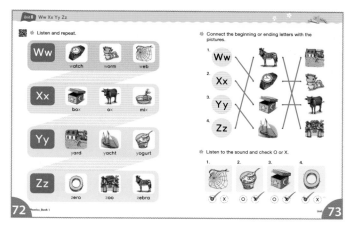

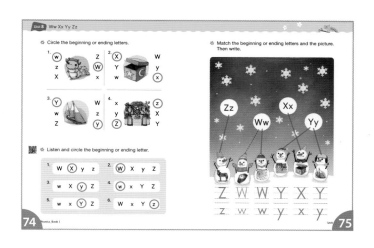

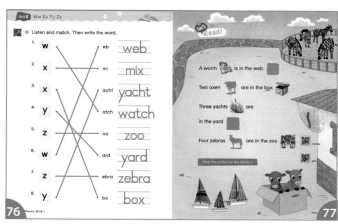

Student Book **Answers**

• Review 2

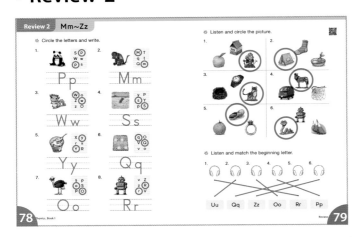

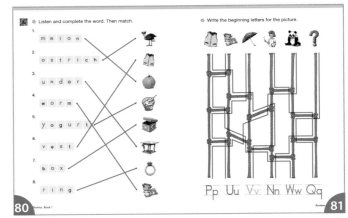

• Final Review

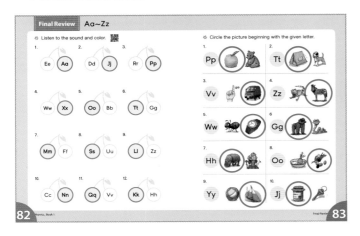

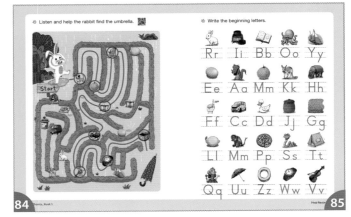

Workbook **Answers**

• Unit 1

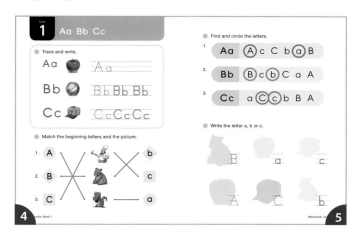

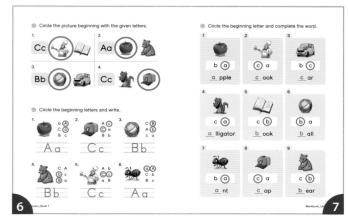

• Unit 2

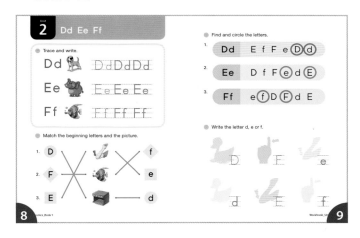

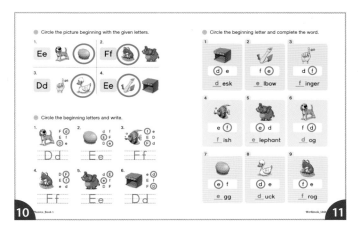

• Unit 3

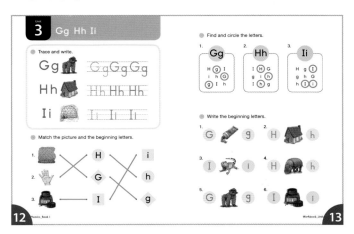

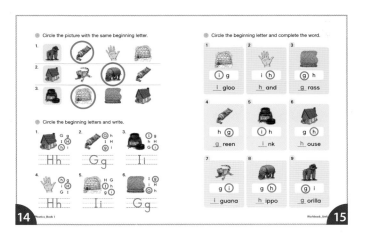

Workbook **Answers**

• Unit 4

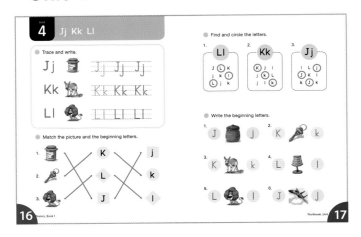
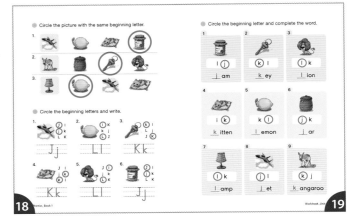

• Review 1

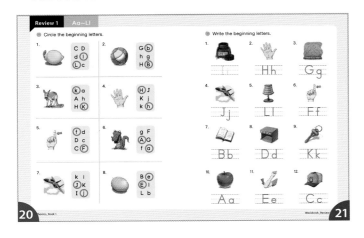
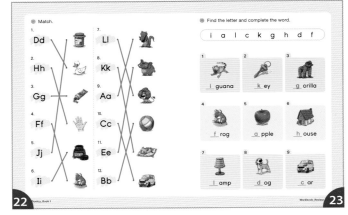

• Unit 5

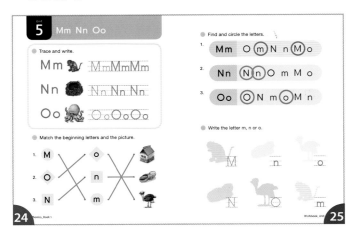
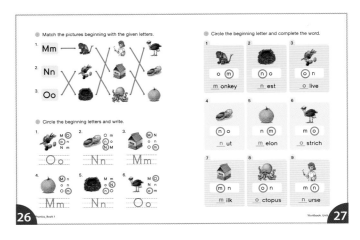

• Unit 6

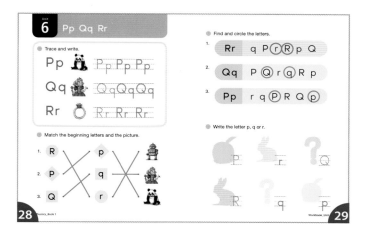

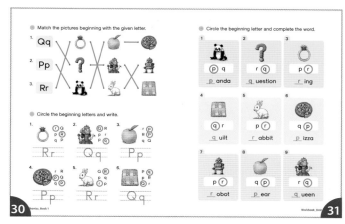

• Unit 7

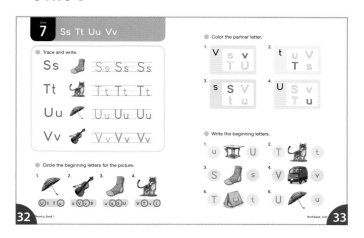

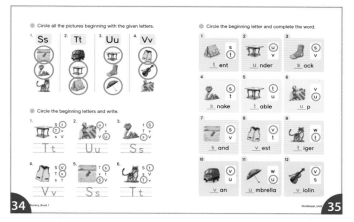

• Unit 8

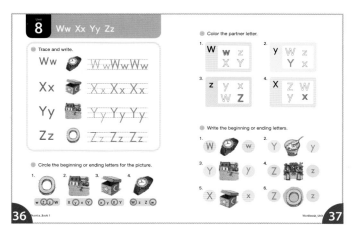

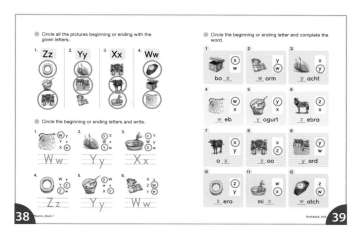

Workbook **Answers**

• Review 2

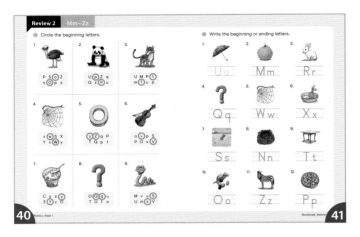

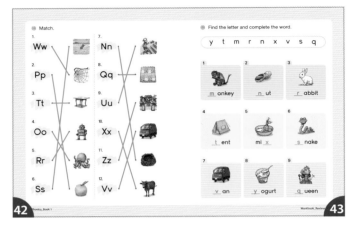

Final Test **Answers**

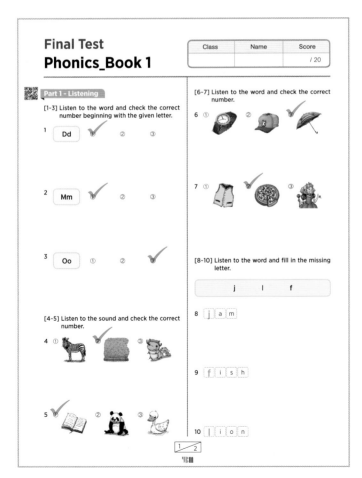

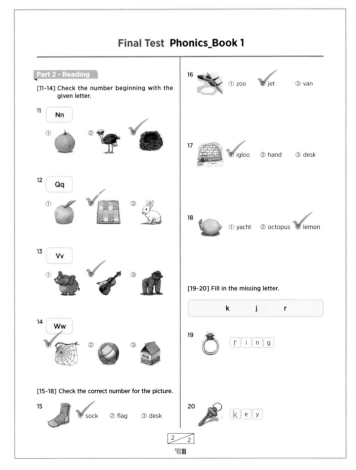

WORD CARDS

Aa

apple

ant

alligator

Bb

bear

book

ball

Cc

car

cap

cook

Dd

dog

duck

desk

Ee

elephant

egg

elbow

Ff

fish

frog

finger

Gg

gorilla

green

grass

Hh

house

hippo

hand

Bb	bear	Aa	apple
	book		ant
	ball		alligator

Dd	dog	Cc	car
	duck		cap
	desk		cook

Ff	fish	Ee	elephant
	frog		egg
	finger		elbow

Hh	house	Gg	gorilla
	hippo		green
	hand		grass

WORD CARDS

I i

igloo

ink

iguana

J j

jam

jet

jar

K k

kangaroo

kitten

key

L l

lion

lemon

lamp

M m

monkey

milk

melon

N n

nest

nut

nurse

O o

octopus

ostrich

olive

P p

panda

pizza

pear

Jj jam jet jar	**Ii** igloo ink iguana
Ll lion lemon lamp	**Kk** kangaroo kitten key
Nn nest nut nurse	**Mm** monkey milk melon
Pp panda pizza pear	**Oo** octopus ostrich olive

WORD CARDS

Qq

 queen

 question

 quilt

Rr

 ring

 rabbit

 robot

Ss

 sock

 snake

 sand

Tt

 tiger

 tent

 table

Uu

 umbrella

 up

 under

Vv

 vest

 violin

 van

Ww

 watch

 worm

 web

Xx

 box

 ox

 mix

Yy

 yard

 yacht

 yogurt

Zz

 zero

 zoo

 zebra

Rr	ring rabbit robot	**Qq**	queen question quilt
Tt	tiger tent table	**Ss**	sock snake sand
Vv	vest violin van	**Uu**	umbrella up under
Xx	box ox mix	**Ww**	watch worm web
Zz	zero zoo zebra	**Yy**	yard yacht yogurt

Unit 1
p.17

Unit 2
p.25

Unit 3
p.33

Unit 4
p.41

Unit 5
p.53

Unit 6
p.61

Unit 7
p.69

Unit 8
p.77

BOOK
1

PHONICS

LAND

Single Letters

WORKBOOK

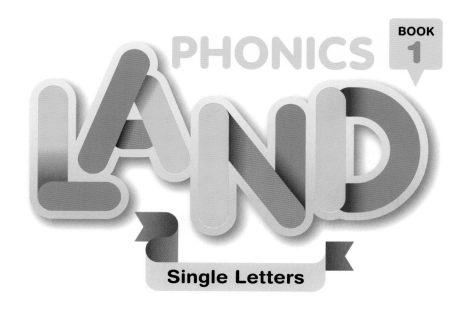

PHONICS **BOOK 1**

LAND

Single Letters

WORKBOOK

YBM

Contents

◎ Trace and write.

Aa ‾A‾a‾‾‾‾‾‾‾‾‾‾

Bb ‾B‾b‾‾‾‾‾‾‾‾‾‾

Cc ‾C‾c‾‾‾‾‾‾‾‾‾‾

◎ Match the beginning letters and the picture.

1. **A** •  • **b**

2. **B** • • **c**

3. **C** • • **a**

🌀 Find and circle the letters.

1. **Aa**   A c C b a B

2. **Bb**   B c b C a A

3. **Cc**   a C c b B A

🌀 Write the letter a, b or c.

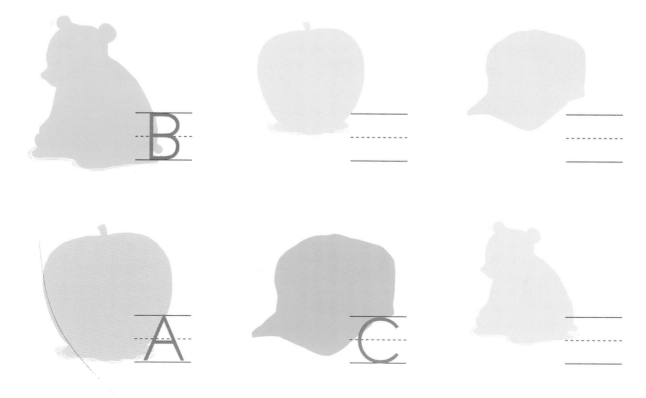

Circle the picture beginning with the given letters.

1. Cc

2. Aa

3. Bb

4. Cc

Circle the beginning letters and write.

1.
b A
C a
B c

_____
_____
_____

2.
A c
C a
B b

_____
_____
_____

3.
C B
A b
c a

_____
_____
_____

4.
C A
b c
B a

_____
_____
_____

5.
A b
C c
a B

_____
_____
_____

6.
a A
C b
B c

_____
_____
_____

🌀 Circle the beginning letter and complete the word.

1

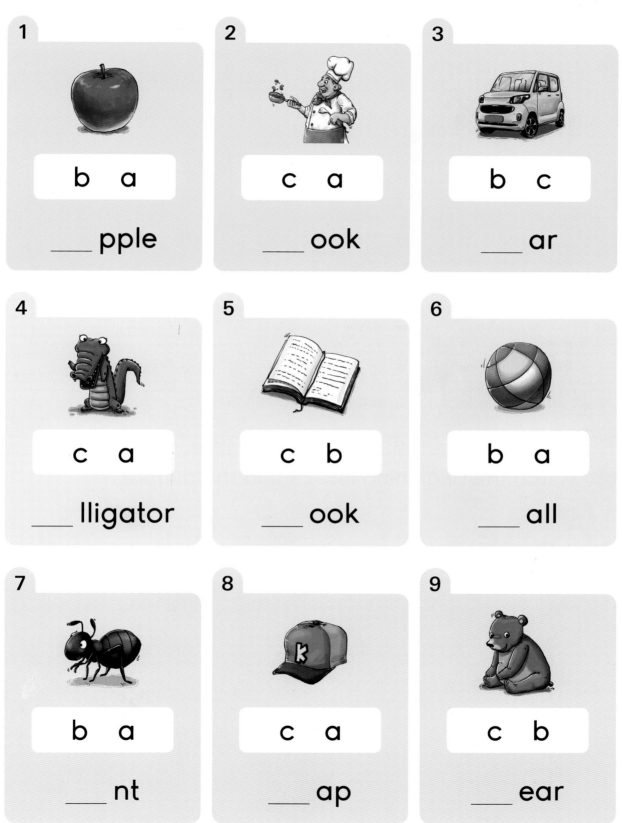

b a

___ pple

2

c a

___ ook

3

b c

___ ar

4

c a

___ lligator

5

c b

___ ook

6

b a

___ all

7

b a

___ nt

8

c a

___ ap

9

c b

___ ear

Trace and write.

D d Dd

E e  Ee

F f  Ff

Match the beginning letters and the picture.

1. D •  • f

2. F •  • e

3. E •  • d

Find and circle the letters.

1. **Dd**   E f F e D d

2. **Ee**   D f F e d E

3. **Ff**   e f D F d E

Write the letter d, e or f.

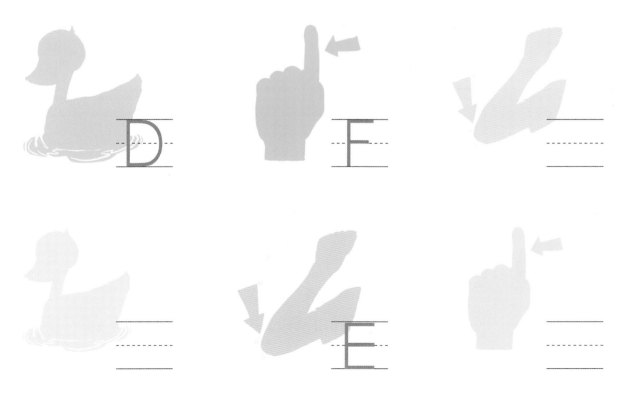

D   E   ___

___   E   ___

Circle the picture beginning with the given letters.

1. **Ee**

2. **Ff**

3. **Dd**

4. **Ee**

Circle the beginning letters and write.

1.
F d
E f
D e

_____

2.
d f
E F
D e

_____

3.
f e
E D
F d

_____

4.
D F
E f
e d

_____

5.
d E
e f
D F

_____

6.
e d
E f
F D

_____

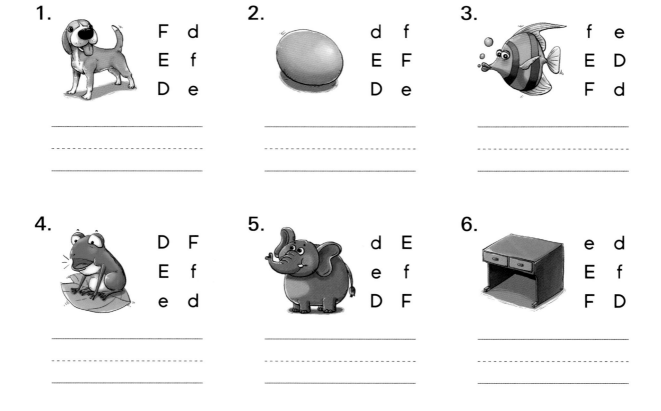

Circle the beginning letter and complete the word.

1
d   e

___esk

2
f   e

___lbow

3
d   f

___inger

4
e   f

___ish

5
e   d

___lephant

6
f   d

___og

7
e   f

___gg

8
d   e

___uck

9
f   e

___rog

Trace and write.

G g     G g

H h     H h

I i     I i

Match the picture and the beginning letters.

1.    H   i

2.    G   h

3.    I   g

Find and circle the letters.

1.
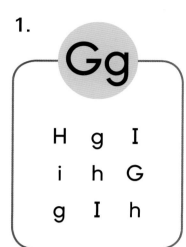
G g

H g I
i h G
g I h

2.
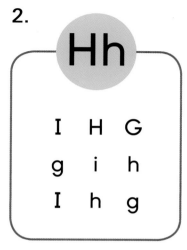
H h

I H G
g i h
I h g

3.
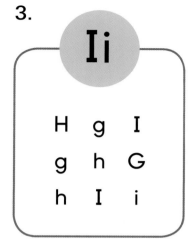
I i

H g I
g h G
h I i

Write the beginning letters.

1.
G

2.
 h

3.
 i

4.
H

5.
 g

6.
I

Circle the picture with the same beginning letter.

1.

2.

3.

 Circle the beginning letters and write.

1.
G g
I H
h i

_____
- - - - - - - - - - - - -
_____

2.
G h
I H
g i

_____
- - - - - - - - - - - - -
_____

3.
I g
h H
G i

_____
- - - - - - - - - - - - -
_____

4.
h g
i H
G I

_____
- - - - - - - - - - - - -
_____

5.
H G
I h
g i

_____
- - - - - - - - - - - - -
_____

6.
I g
i H
G h

_____
- - - - - - - - - - - - -
_____

Circle the beginning letter and complete the word.

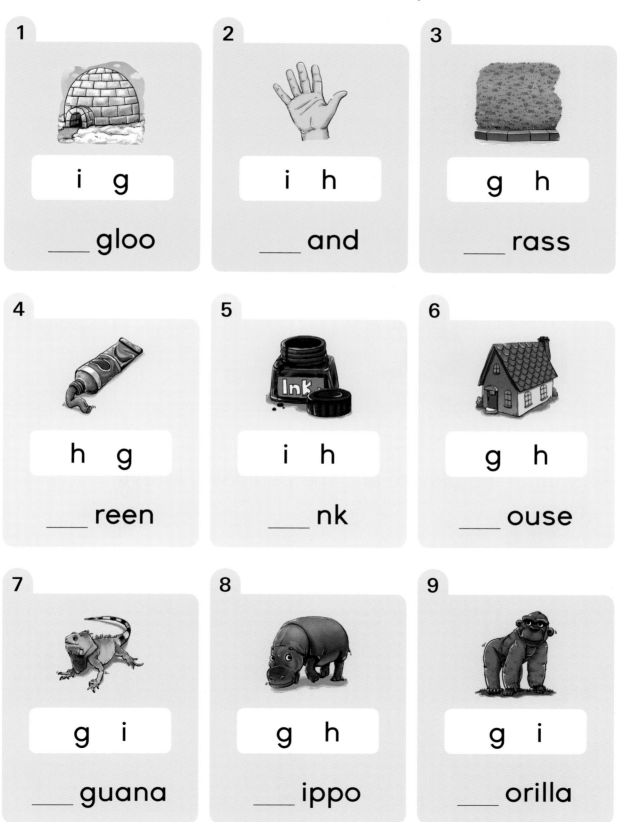

1 i g

___ gloo

2 i h

___ and

3 g h

___ rass

4 h g

___ reen

5 i h

___ nk

6 g h

___ ouse

7 g i

___ guana

8 g h

___ ippo

9 g i

___ orilla

🌀 Trace and write.

J j Jj

Kk  Kk

Ll Ll

🌀 Match the picture and the beginning letters.

1. • • **K** • • **j**

2.  • • **L** • • **k**

3.  • **J** • • **l**

Find and circle the letters.

1.
Ll

J	L	K
j	k	l
L	j	k

2.
Kk

K	J	l
j	k	L
j	l	k

3.
Jj

l	L	j
J	K	l
k	J	k

Write the beginning letters.

1.

2. K

3.  k

4. l

5. L

6. J

Circle the picture with the same beginning letter.

1.

2.

3.

Circle the beginning letters and write.

1.
J   l
j   k
L   K

_____

- - - - - - - - - - - - - - -

_____

2.
l   K
k   j
L   J

_____

- - - - - - - - - - - - - - -

_____

3.
k   l
L   j
J   K

_____

- - - - - - - - - - - - - - -

_____

4.
J   l
j   k
K   l

_____

- - - - - - - - - - - - - - -

_____

5.
J   l
j   k
L   K

_____

- - - - - - - - - - - - - - -

_____

6.
J   l
j   k
L   K

_____

- - - - - - - - - - - - - - -

_____

Circle the beginning letter and complete the word.

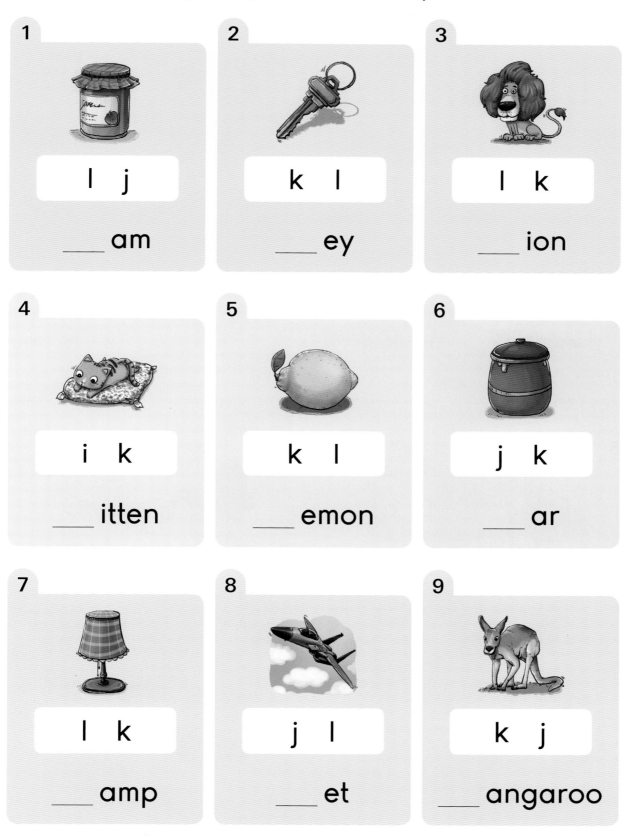

1

l   j

___ am

2

k   l

___ ey

3

l   k

___ ion

4

i   k

___ itten

5

k   l

___ emon

6

j   k

___ ar

7

l   k

___ amp

8

j   l

___ et

9

k   j

___ angaroo

Circle the beginning letters.

1.

C D
d l
L c

2.

G b
h g
H B

3.

k a
A h
H K

4.

H J
K j
k h

5.

f d
D c
C F

6.

g F
A G
f a

7.

k i
J K
I j

8.

B e
E l
L b

Write the beginning letters.

1.

I i

2.

3.

4.

5.

6.

7.

8.

9.

10.

11.

12.

◎ Match.

1.

Dd •

•

7.

Ll •

•

2.

Hh •

•

8.

Kk •

•

3.

Gg •

•

9.

Aa •

•

4.

Ff •

•

10.

Cc •

•

5.

Jj •

•

11.

Ee •

•

6.

Ii •

•

12.

Bb •

•

Find the letter and complete the word.

i a l c k g h d f

1 ___ guana

2 ___ ey

3 ___ orilla

4 ___ rog

5 ___ pple

6 ___ ouse

7 ___ amp

8 ___ og

9 ___ ar

Trace and write.

M m  Mm

N n  Nn

O o  Oo

Match the beginning letters and the picture.

1. **M** ·   · **o** ·   ·

2. **O** ·   · **n** ·   ·

3. **N** ·   · **m** ·   ·

Find and circle the letters.

1.
Mm O m N n M o

2.
Nn N n O m M o

3.
Oo O N m o M n

Write the letter m, n or o.

Match the pictures beginning with the given letters.

1. **Mm** •   •   •   •

2. **Nn** •   •   •   •

3. **Oo** •   •   •   •

Circle the beginning letters and write.

1.
M O
o n
N m

_____
- - - - - - - - - - -
_____

2.
O m
n o
N M

_____
- - - - - - - - - - -
_____

3.
M N
o n
O m

_____
- - - - - - - - - - -
_____

4.
M n
o n
O m

_____
- - - - - - - - - - -
_____

5.
M m
o N
n O

_____
- - - - - - - - - - -
_____

6.
M O
N n
o m

_____
- - - - - - - - - - -
_____

Circle the beginning letter and complete the word.

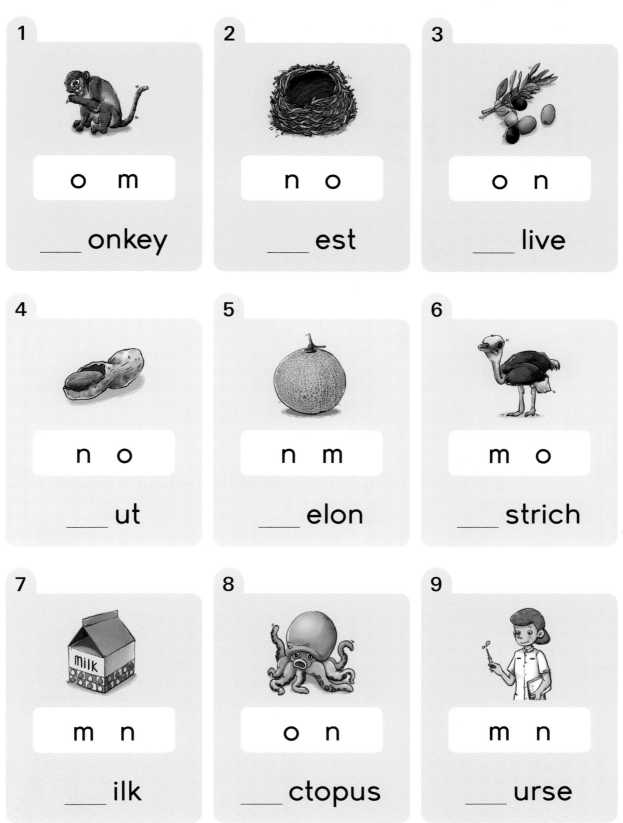

1　o　m　___onkey

2　n　o　___est

3　o　n　___live

4　n　o　___ut

5　n　m　___elon

6　m　o　___strich

7　m　n　___ilk

8　o　n　___ctopus

9　m　n　___urse

◎ Trace and write.

P p  Pp

Q q  Qq

R r Rr

◎ Match the beginning letters and the picture.

1. **R** • • **p** •

2. **P** • • **q** •

3. **Q** • • **r** •

Find and circle the letters.

1.
Rr   q P r R p Q

2.
Qq   P P Q r q R p

3.
Pp   r q P R Q p

Write the letter p, q or r.

Match the pictures beginning with the given letter.

1. **Qq** • •  •  •

2. **Pp** • • •  •

3. **Rr** • •  •  •

Circle the beginning letters and write.

1.

r	Q
p	R
q	P

_____
- - - - - - - - - - - - - - -
_____

2.

Q	R
p	r
P	q

_____
- - - - - - - - - - - - - - -
_____

3.

r	p
R	P
q	Q

_____
- - - - - - - - - - - - - - -
_____

4.

r	R
p	Q
q	P

_____
- - - - - - - - - - - - - - -
_____

5.

Q	R
p	q
r	p

_____
- - - - - - - - - - - - - - -
_____

6.

P	q
p	R
Q	r

_____
- - - - - - - - - - - - - - -
_____

Circle the beginning letter and complete the word.

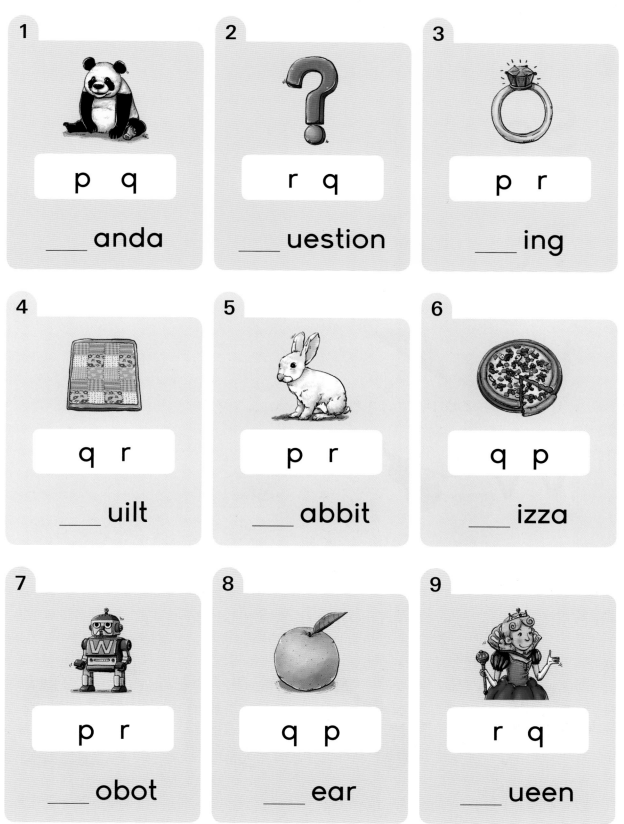

1
p q

___ anda

2
r q

___ uestion

3
p r

___ ing

4
q r

___ uilt

5
p r

___ abbit

6
q p

___ izza

7
p r

___ obot

8
q p

___ ear

9
r q

___ ueen

Ss Tt Uu Vv

◎ Trace and write.

S s

S s

T t

T t

U u

U u

V v

V v

◎ Circle the beginning letters for the picture.

1.

U t **T** u

2.

s **V** v S

3.

u s **S** U

4.

V **T** v t

Color the partner letter.

1.

V

S	V
T	U

2.

t

u	V
T	s

3.

s

S	V
t	u

4.

U

S	V
T	u

Write the beginning letters.

1.

u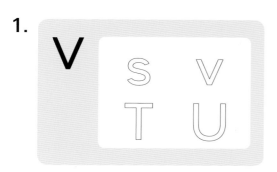

2.

T

3.

 s

4.

V

5.

 t

6.

 u

 Circle all the pictures beginning with the given letters.

1. **Ss**

2. **Tt**

3. **Uu**

4. **Vv**

Circle the beginning letters and write.

1.

S t
T v
s V

_____

- - - - - - - - - - -

_____

2.

u t
T v
V U

_____

- - - - - - - - - - -

_____

3.

t S
T v
s V

_____

- - - - - - - - - - -

_____

4.

S V
T v
s t

_____

- - - - - - - - - - -

_____

5.

T s
v t
S V

_____

- - - - - - - - - - -

_____

6.

S t
s V
T v

_____

- - - - - - - - - - -

_____

Circle the beginning letter and complete the word.

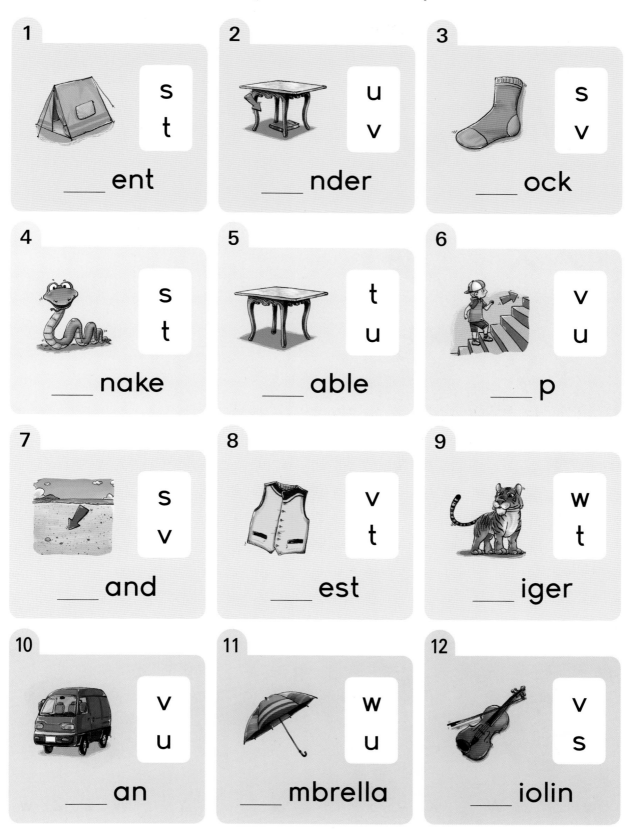

1
s
t
___ent

2
u
v
___nder

3
s
v
___ock

4
s
t
___nake

5
t
u
___able

6
v
u
___p

7
s
v
___and

8
v
t
___est

9
w
t
___iger

10
v
u
___an

11
w
u
___mbrella

12
v
s
___iolin

◎ Trace and write.

Ww

Xx

Yy

Zz

◎ Circle the beginning or ending letters for the picture.

1.

w Z z W

2.

X y x Y

3.

x y X Y

4.

W z Z w

Color the partner letter.

1.
W
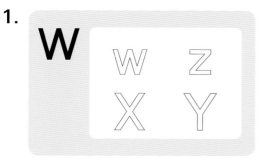
w   z
X   Y

2.
y
W   z
Y   x

3.
z
y   x
W   Z

4.
X
Z   W
y   x

Write the beginning or ending letters.

1.

w

2.
Y

3.

y

4.

z

5.
X

6.
Z

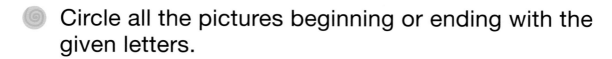 Circle all the pictures beginning or ending with the given letters.

1. **Zz**	2. **Yy**	3. **Xx**	4. **Ww**

Circle the beginning or ending letters and write.

1.    W y
            Y x
            X w

_____
- - - - - - - - - - - -
_____

2.    y X
            W x
            Y w

_____
- - - - - - - - - - - -
_____

3.    x Y
            W y
            X w

_____
- - - - - - - - - - - -
_____

4.   W y
            Y z
            Z w

_____
- - - - - - - - - - - -
_____

5.    y W
            w x
            X Y

_____
- - - - - - - - - - - -
_____

6.    X z
            Z W
            x w

_____
- - - - - - - - - - - -
_____

Circle the beginning or ending letter and complete the word.

1
x
w
bo ___

2
y
w
___ orm

3
x
y
___ acht

4
w
x
___ eb

5
y
x
___ ogurt

6
z
x
___ ebra

7
x
y
o ___

8
x
z
___ oo

9
y
w
___ ard

10
z
y
___ ero

11
w
x
mi ___

12
z
w
___ atch

🌀 Circle the beginning letters.

1.

P S o Z
s O p z

2.

U p Z q
Q z P u

3.

U M P t
m T u p

4.

x w S X
Y s W y

5.

z Z q P
T Q p t

6.

o v p S
P O s V

7.

C o z y
Z Y c O

8.

O Q q u
T U t o

9.

M v u S
U m s V

Write the beginning or ending letters.

1.

U u

2.

3.

4.

5.

6.

7.

8.

9.

10.

11.

12.

@ Match.

1.

Ww •

•

2.

Pp •

•

3.

Tt •

•

4.

Oo •

•

5.

Rr •

•

6.

Ss •

•

7.

Nn •

•

8.

Qq •

•

9.

Uu •

•

10.

Xx •

•

11.

Zz •

•

12.

Vv •

•

Find the letter and complete the word.

y t m r n x v s q

1

___ onkey

2

___ ut

3

___ abbit

4

___ ent

5

mi ___

6

___ nake

7

___ an

8

___ ogurt

9

___ ueen

Memo

Final Test
Phonics_Book 1

Class	Name	Score
		/ 20

[1~3] Listen to the word and check the correct number beginning with the given letter.

1 Dd ① ② ③

2 Mm ① ② ③

3 Oo ① ② ③

[4~5] Listen to the sound and check the correct number.

4 ①   ②   ③

5 ①   ②   ③

[6~7] Listen to the word and check the correct number.

6 ①   ②   ③

7 ①   ②   ③

[8~10] Listen to the word and fill in the missing letter.

j	l	f

8 ☐ a m

9 ☐ i s h

10 ☐ i o n

Final Test Phonics_Book 1

[11~14] Check the number beginning with the given letter.

11 Nn

①    ②   ③

12 Qq

①    ② 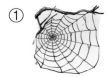   ③

13 Vv

①   ②   ③

14 Ww

①   ②   ③ milk

[15~18] Check the correct number for the picture.

15 ① sock   ② flag   ③ desk

16 ① zoo   ② jet   ③ van

17 ① igloo   ② hand   ③ desk

18 ① yacht   ② octopus   ③ lemon

[19~20] Fill in the missing letter.

k   j   r

19 ☐ i n g

20 ☐ e y

2 / 2

YBM